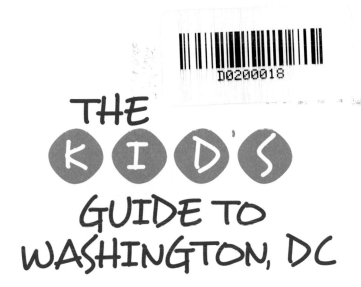

THE KID'S GUIDE TO WASHINGTON, DC

D0200018

THE KID'S GUIDE TO WASHINGTON, DC

1st edition

Eileen Ogintz

gpp® travel

Guilford, Connecticut

Thanks to Meghan McCloskey and Jonathan Boydston
for their research help in Washington, DC,
especially interviewing local and visiting kids, and to
Melissa Miller, a teacher, for contributing the games.

All the information in this guidebook is subject to change.
We recommend that you call ahead to obtain current
information before traveling.

Distributed by NATIONAL BOOK NETWORK

Illustrations licensed by Shutterstock.com

ISBN 978-0-7627-8647-3

Printed in the United States of America

Contents

1

Welcome to the Nation's Capital!

Virginia or New York?

The Founding Fathers couldn't agree on whether the new nation's capital would be in the North or the South. Alexander Hamilton, a northerner, and Thomas Jefferson, from Virginia, came up with the idea to build the new city right on the border between the North and South. They left it up to President George Washington to figure out where. Washington zeroed in on an area on the Potomac River just 20 miles from his Mount Vernon estate in Virginia; Maryland and Virginia agreed to give land so the city could be built. Construction began in 1793 on the president's house and the Capitol. But work was just barely done when the British marched in in August 1814

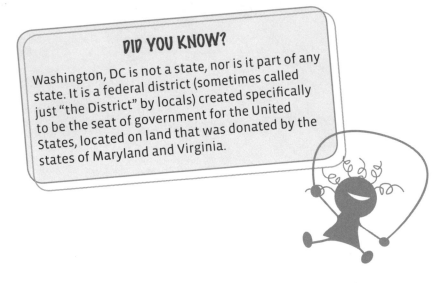

DID YOU KNOW?

Washington, DC is not a state, nor is it part of any state. It is a federal district (sometimes called just "the District" by locals) created specifically to be the seat of government for the United States, located on land that was donated by the states of Maryland and Virginia.

and burned most of the city's government buildings. In the aftermath, Congress nearly voted to leave for another city. We're glad they didn't because today Washington, DC is a standout with gleaming monuments, great museums, the National Zoo, good eats, and hundreds of acres of parks and wetlands. But this city is more than monuments and museums. You will meet people from all around the country and the world here—including lots of kids—whose parents work for the government, foreign embassies, and the media. There are a lot of reporters and editors here!

Many neighborhoods are fun to explore. The hard part is figuring out which one to explore first!

- **Woodley Park/Cleveland Park** is north of Dupont Circle and home to the famous National Zoo, Rock Creek Park, and the National Cathedral. These neighborhoods once were suburbs.

DID YOU KNOW?
DC welcomes approximately 16 million visitors each year.

- **U Street/Shaw/Logan Circle** is home to the African American Civil War Memorial, the Lincoln Theatre, and Howard University as well as Ben's Chili Bowl, which is great for lunch if you like chili. Here's where you can follow the steps of famous jazz musicians like Duke Ellington.

- **Southwest/Waterfront** is southwest of the National Mall to the Washington Channel. This is where the Nationals play baseball! The longest operating fish market in the United States is here too—the Maine Avenue Fish Market.

- **Georgetown** is bordered by Wisconsin Avenue and M Street NW and by the Potomac to the south. It's been around since 1751, and you'll see lots of old houses, restaurants, shops, and Georgetown University here. Check out the gardens at Dumbarton Oaks (doaks.org/gardens).

DID YOU KNOW?

Georgetown wasn't named for George Washington and might even have been named for King George II of England or other town founders named George.

- **Foggy Bottom** is between the White House and Georgetown. It's named for the fog that used to rise up from the Potomac River. There are lots of fancy hotels here as well as the Kennedy Center, the Department of State, and George Washington University.

- **Dupont Circle/Kalorama** includes Connecticut, Massachusetts, and New Hampshire Avenues at P and 19th Streets. The Circle is named for Civil War naval hero Rear Admiral Samuel Francis Dupont. If you like chess, you can join a pickup game in the circle. Stop at the neighborhood farmers' market on Sunday (fresh farmmarkets.org) or check out one of the restaurants with food from around the world. Along Embassy Row on Massachusetts Avenue, you can see many embassies for nations from around the world.

- **Downtown DC** is where you'll find cool museums like the International Spy Museum, Newseum, and Madame Tussauds. The Verizon Center here hosts college and pro sports as well as concerts (verizoncenter .com).

- **Capitol Hill** is east of the Capitol Dome. You'll come here to visit the Library of Congress, the Supreme Court, the National Postal Museum, and Union Station. You can also visit Eastern Market on Saturday, Sunday, or Tuesday for fresh food, music, and arts and crafts (easternmarket-dc.org).

A VISITING KID SAYS:
"What surprised me the most about Washington, DC was how many people there were that were from different countries. I was also surprised at how many historical events took place there."
—Greta, 11, Boise, ID

- **Brookland/Northeast** is northeast of the Capitol and is sometimes called "Little Rome" because it has more than 60 Catholic sites including Catholic University of America. Check out the National Arboretum's huge herb garden (usna.usda.gov)!

- **Anacostia** is southeast of the Capitol and across the 11th Street Bridge. It's named for a Native American tribe and is where abolitionist Frederick Douglass lived. You can visit his estate, Cedar Hill (nps.gov/frdo), or learn about African-American history at the Smithsonian's Anacostia Community Museum.

Good Eats

You can get any kind of food you like in Washington, DC. These are some places to try:

Ben's Chili Bowl (1213 U St. NW; 202-667-0909; benschili bowl.com) is famous for chili dogs and milk shakes.

Carmine's (425 7th St. NW; 202-737-7770; carminesnyc .com) for huge portions of your favorite pastas.

Comet Ping Pong (5037 Connecticut Ave. NW; 202-364-0404; cometpingpong.com) invites customers to play a game of table tennis while waiting for pizza from the wood-fired oven.

Eastern Market (225 7th St. SE; 202-698-5253; eastern market-dc.org) is famous for its blueberry buckwheat pancakes on Saturday mornings.

Firefly (1310 New Hampshire Ave. NW; 202-861-1310; fire fly-dc.com) will make you feel like you're eating in the middle of a forest and has a really great kids' menu. Littler kids get to decorate a cookie!

Founding Farmers (1924 Pennsylvania Ave. NW; 202-822-8783; wearefoundingfarmers.com) is known for food made with fresh ingredients from local farmers like "popcorn of the day," southern pan-fried chicken, and waffles.

Hill Country BBQ (410 7th St. NW; 202-556-2050; hill countryny.com) is a Texas-style barbecue restaurant that is like an old-style meat market where guests order from different counters and then pay up at the end. You can always go back for seconds!

Tackle Box (3245 M St. NW; 202-337-8269; tacklebox restaurant.com) offers fresh seafood and claims the city's best blueberry pie.

Tony Cheng's (619 H St. NW; 202-371-8669; tonychengs restaurant.com) offers half-price plates for kids under 12.

Z Burger (4321 Wisconsin Ave. NW, 2414 Wisconsin Ave. NW, 1101 4th St. SW; zburger.com) is local burger joint that has more than just burgers—there's 75 flavors of milk shakes!

Let the Metro Be Your Guide

You not only will be traveling greener leaving your car at the hotel, but you'll get around the District the way locals do because on-street parking is limited and finding a spot can be frustrating. The **Metro** (wmata.com) is convenient, safe, and clean. You can get a daily unlimited or weekly pass. There is also a **DC Circulator bus** (dccirculator.com) that connects DC neighborhoods for just $1 a trip. Tell your parents you'll navigate, using the free Trip Planner on a smartphone or computer: Type in where you're traveling from and where you're going, and the Trip Planner will tell you how to get there. You can also opt for a tour (dctours.us) that allows you to get on and off the bus at all of the major sites and stay as long as you like, catching the next bus, or see the sights aboard the **Old Town Trolley** (trolleytours.com/washington-dc/index.asp).

DID YOU KNOW?

Kids from all over the world live in Washington, DC. That's because the District is home to more than 150 embassies, chanceries, and international cultural centers, some of which are open regularly to the public. You can visit embassies from around the world, welcoming visitors with music, dance, food, and more during Passport DC (culturaltourismdc.org).

What's Cool? You can join the famous Drum Circle at Meridian Hill Park starting at 3 p.m. on Sunday. E-mail William H. Taft, the drum circle's sponsor, at drumcircle .talkindrum@gmail.com for more information. Just bring your own drum!

National Cathedral

Ready for a scavenger hunt? This one is in a church—a huge church: the **National Cathedral** (Massachusetts and Wisconsin Avenues, NW; 202-537-6200; nationalcathedral.org). You can find images in the stained-glass windows, wrought-iron animals, tiny carvings, and gargoyles. (Look for the hunt brochure on the information table when you arrive.) Don't miss the Children's Chapel with its kid-size chairs and pipe organ. This church is big! There are 233 stained-glass windows, a 10,250-pipe organ (check out a free organ demonstration on Monday and Wednesday afternoons), nine chapels, and even a piece of moon rock brought back by astronauts Neil Armstrong and Buzz Aldrin. The ceiling

is 100 feet high! Its official name is the Cathedral Church of St. Peter and St. Paul, but everyone calls it the National Cathedral. Check out the big stone gargoyles and grotesques that decorate the National Cathedral. (What's the difference? Grotesques are distorted or fantastic human and animal forms used as decorations; gargoyles are grotesques with water spouts.) Climb the 333 steps to the heights of the bell-ringing chamber in the great central tower—300 feet above the ground (there are recitals of the bells on Saturday afternoons)—and take a walk through the huge Bishop's Garden. There are special family workshops on certain Saturdays too. You've seen this church on TV. It has been the location of funeral and memorial services for 15 presidents and where presidential interfaith services typically are held after the inauguration. The cathedral was damaged during the 2011 earthquake. Can you see where? Repairs will go on for years!

There may be more free things to do in Washington, DC than any other city because so many of the city's museums and attractions are free. Here are seven picks for families you might not know about:

- **African American Heritage Trail.** Explore the trail to learn about both popular and lesser-known sites of significance to DC's black history (culturaltourismdc.org/things-do-see/tours-trails/african-american-heritage-trail-washington-dc).

- **John F. Kennedy Center for the Performing Arts.** Catch a free performance daily at 6 p.m. at the Kennedy Center's Millennium Stage (kennedy-center.org/programs/millennium).

- **Rock Creek Park.** Run, walk, or bike on 1,754 acres of rustic woodlands showing the best of DC's green side (nps.gov/rocr/planyourvisit/index .htm).

- **Smithsonian American Art Museum.** Enjoy free, live jazz at the "Take Five!" performance series. It usually happens on the third Thursday of each month, and the museum's cafe stays open so guests can enjoy beer, wine, and light snacks during the performance (americanart.si.edu/calendar/performances/music/five).

- **Supreme Court of the United States.** Watch history being made by sitting in on a Supreme Court ruling (supremecourt.gov/visiting/visiting.aspx).

- **The National Gallery of Art Sculpture Garden.** Have a picnic and listen to music at the Jazz in the Garden concert series every Friday evening in the summer (nga.gov/programs/jazz).

- **U Street Corridor.** Walk in the footsteps of great jazz musicians in this neighborhood, also known as "Black Broadway." Here you'll find the African American Civil War Memorial, the famous Ben's Chili Bowl, and signs for Cultural Tourism DC's self-guided walking tour to help you find your way (culturaltourismdc.org/things-do-see/historic-neighborhoods/greater-u-street).

Union Station

Quick, where can you grab some sushi, catch a train, buy a souvenir, see a movie, or learn a little history? Washington, DC's **Union Station** (Massachusetts Avenue and North Capitol St.; 202-289-1908; unionstationdc.com) of course! This is where soldiers traditionally have passed through on their way to war. The Main Hall is huge! There are 130 stores (including the Great Train Store), and in the food court, take your pick of BBQ, wraps, smoothies, or pizza. More than 90,000 visitors pass through Union Station's doors daily. Check out the figures of Roman legionnaires around the ledge of the balcony in the Main Hall. The figures were originally cast as nudes, but railroad officials, fearing the public would be offended, ordered shields be strategically placed on each statue. You can still see those shields today. Union Station opened in 1907 and has been part of US history ever since—even setting the tone for the design of the famous monuments like the Lincoln and Jefferson Memorials and Supreme Court Building you'll see during your visit. It was restored in the 1980s at a cost of more than $100 million. Now Union Station has just undergone another renovation to repair significant damage caused by the August 23, 2011, earthquake, the most violent recorded quake to strike Washington, DC, which caused sections of ceiling plaster to crumble and break free from the Main Hall and Concourse area.

INTERNATIONAL FLAGS

There are so many embassies housing diplomats from other countries around DC. Draw some of the flags you see in the space below! Make sure to label your drawings so you don't forget which country each flag belongs to!

2

The Monuments

We've had 44 presidents,

but only four have been honored with monuments. You are going to visit them here in Washington, DC right on the National Mall.

THE WASHINGTON MONUMENT

The Washington Monument is 555 feet, 5 inches high! Did you know the giant obelisk is only 18 inches wide at the top? It took nearly 50 years to get the monument built. Check out how the stones get darker the higher they are. That's because the project took so long to finish that the marble came from another part of the quarry and was a slightly different shade (nps.gov/wamo).

THE LINCOLN MEMORIAL

A lot of people like to visit the Lincoln Memorial at night because it is so beautiful and you might be able to see across the Potomac to Arlington National Cemetery. It took 28 blocks of marble to carve this giant 19-foot por- trait of Abraham Lincoln. Look for the words of Lincoln's Gettysburg Address and his Second Inaugural Address carved in the walls (nps .gov/linc).

THE THOMAS JEFFERSON MEMORIAL

Jefferson was one of the Founding Fathers and the third president of the United States from 1801 to 1809. But it took 135 years before he was honored with this monument. If you think it looks familiar, Jefferson used the design of a round building with a dome at the University of Virginia and his home in Virginia. The famous Pantheon in Rome has a similar rotunda design. Check out the carved inscriptions of his writings. Can you find the mistakes in the Declaration of Independence (nps.gov/thje)?

A LOCAL KID SAYS:
"The best souvenir from Washington, DC is a mini Washington Monument."
—William, 12, Potomac, MD

DID YOU KNOW?
Above the Lincoln Memorial's 38 columns are the names of the 36 states that were in the Union at the time of his death.

FRANKLIN DELANO ROOSEVELT MEMORIAL

The Franklin Delano Roosevelt Memorial is the newest of the presidential monuments (it was opened in 1997). Check out the sculpture of FDR with his dog Fala (3 feet high!). Stop in at the information center where you might see a replica of the wheelchair FDR designed and used himself—he suffered from polio (nps.gov/fdrm).

MARTIN LUTHER KING JR. MEMORIAL

The Stone of Hope is the central point of the MLK Memorial (nps.gov/mlkm). If you are lucky enough to visit in April, you'll see some of the city's famous cherry trees in bloom.

DID YOU KNOW?

The Martin Luther King Jr. Memorial on the National Mall is the newest monument in the area. It was unveiled in August 2011, the 48th anniversary of his "I Have a Dream" speech in Washington, DC. It is the first memorial on the Mall not dedicated to a war, a president, or a white man.

WAR MEMORIALS

While you are here, you'll also visit the famous war memorials. There's one for World War II veterans, Korean War veterans, and Vietnam veterans.

Look at the mural wall at the Korean War Veterans Memorial (nps.gov/kowa). The faces were made from photos of soldiers in that war.

The World War II Memorial honors the 16 million who served during World War II—soldiers as well as those at home. See the 4,000 gold stars? They represent the 400,000 American soldiers who died during the war. A soldier's mom would put a gold star in the window to tell people she had lost a son. Can you count the 56 granite pillars? They represent each state, territory, and the District of Columbia and are arranged according to the year they entered the union (nps.gov/nwwm).

A LOCAL KID SAYS:
"On a rainy day, bring an umbrella and go to the National Mall. Nobody's there!"
—Sean, 11, Arlington, VA

The Vietnam Veterans Memorial has become one of the most visited sites in Washington, DC, and friends and relatives of those whose names you can read sometimes leave mementos. It's sad to think of all of the people who died fighting. But it makes you proud too (nps.gov/vive).

A VISITING KID SAYS:
"My favorite place that I visited in Washington, DC was the Lincoln Memorial. I enjoyed reading the quotes on the walls and seeing the architecture based off of intertwined cultures."
—Hayley, 13, Fort Worth, TX

DID YOU KNOW?
The gloves of the soldiers who guard the Tomb of the Unknowns at Arlington National Cemetery may seem wet. Before standing guard, they soak their gloves to better grip the wood handle of their rifle. The changing of the guard takes place every half hour from April through September and every hour on the hour from October until March.

Arlington National Cemetery

When you visit **Arlington National Cemetery** (arlington cemetery.mil), you realize the price we all pay for war. More than 300,000 of those who died fighting for our country are buried here just across the Potomac from Washington. It is the largest military cemetery in the country. President John F. Kennedy, his wife, Jacqueline Kennedy Onassis, and two of their children are buried here, as are Senator Robert Kennedy and Senator Edward M. Kennedy. President Kennedy and President William Howard Taft are the only presidents buried at Arlington. You can visit the graves of civil rights hero Medgar Evers, Supreme Court justices Thurgood Marshall and Oliver Wendell Holmes, and unknown soldiers in the Tomb of the Unknowns, which is guarded 24 hours a day (you will want to watch the changing of the guard).

There's a Women in Military Service for America Memorial and the famous statue of the Marines raising the flag over Iwo Jima at the Marine Corps War Memorial. The US Marine Drum and Bugle Corps perform at the memorial in summer (nps.gov/gwmp). You can climb the tower of the 49-bell carillon nearby. Just leave your car at the hotel. It's much easier to take the Metro here or to take Tourmobile (tourmobile.com), which allows you to get on and off at the Mall and goes to Arlington National Cemetery.

TELL THE ADULTS:

Historical monuments can be boring! But they don't have to be. Here's how to make a visit more fun:

- Read a kid's book about the president whose memorial you are going to visit. Have some fun facts at hand. (George Washington probably never chopped down a cherry tree. The story was invented by a man who wrote a biography of Washington shortly after he died.)

- Bring a Frisbee or ball to play with on the National Mall.

- Assign each member of the family to reveal one fun fact about the president whose monument you are visiting. (You can find out plenty by visiting nps.gov/nama.)

A VISITING KID SAYS:
"My favorite memory from Washington, DC was visiting all the monuments in the dark. They were all lit up beautifully."
—Greta, 11, Boise, ID

- At the National Mall and Memorial Parks, kids can become a junior ranger and earn their very own junior ranger badge (nps.gov/nama/forkids/beajuniorranger.htm)!

- There is an app that you can use to explore the National Mall (nps.gov/nama/photosmultimedia/app-page.htm).

- Use the opportunity for visiting the war memorials to tell kids what life was like for American kids during that era—Vietnam, WWII, etc.

DID YOU KNOW?

The statue of Eleanor Roosevelt at the Franklin Delano Roosevelt Memorial is the only monumental tribute to a first lady. She's standing in front of the United Nations emblem because she helped create the United Nations.

National Mall

Welcome to America's front yard. That's what a lot of people call the **National Mall.** Bet it's a lot bigger than your yard— it's 3 miles long, stretching from the Potomac River in the west to Capitol Hill in the east. This is where you find the Carousel and Smithsonian Museums, the famous Reflecting Pool, and Tidal Basin Boathouse, memorials to those who died in wars and to presidents. This is also where the historic 1963 March on Washington ended with Martin Luther King Jr.'s famous "I Have a Dream" speech. A lot of people listened sitting around and even in the Reflecting Pool. You can fly kites here (there is a group event, in fact, at the Washington Monument on the day of the annual Smithsonian Kite Festival, usually in late spring), turn cartwheels, race your brother, get a hot dog, or buy a souvenir. In July, there's a big Folklife Festival with lots of fun things for kids to do. If you're here on the Fourth of July, you can watch the fireworks. Check out nps.gov/nama to find out what's going on during your visit. Attend a concert or a rally. Bring a picnic. Just make sure you wear comfy shoes. You're going to do a lot of walking— and running—here.

DID YOU KNOW?

There is no fee to visit any part of the National Mall and Memorial Parks, and they are open 24 hours a day.

Can you unscramble these words related to the Washington, DC monuments?

LCONILN

— — — — — — —

CRINGFLEET POLO

— — — — — — — — — — — —

IARTMN UHTLRE GKNI RJ

— — — — — — — — — — — — — — — — — —

NOEAELR SLTEVEOOR

— — — — — — — — — — — — — —

TWSNAIGHON

— — — — — — — — — —

NGNTOLARI MEEERYTC

— — — — — — — — — — — — — — — —

RHEYCR LSOSMSOB

— — — — — — — — — — — — —

EIKT VASETIFL

— — — — — — — — — — —

FREOSNEJF

— — — — — — — — —

DROWL RAW II

— — — — — — — — —

See page 152 for the answers!

3

Ruby Slippers,
Moon Rocks & Dinosaurs—
The Smithsonian

Ready to touch a piece of the moon?

You can at the National Air and Space Museum, the Smithsonian's most popular venue (4th Street and Independence Avenue SW; airandspace.si.edu). Welcome to the most visited museum in the world!

In fact, you'll see families from around the world at the National Air and Space Museum as well as the National Museum of American History (don't miss the Star-Spangled Banner that inspired our national anthem at 14th Street and Constitution Avenue NW; 202-633-1000; americanhistory.si.edu) and the National Museum of Natural History (10th Street NW and Constitution Avenue; 202-633-1000; nmnh.si.edu). Want to crawl through a termite mound?

DID YOU KNOW?

The Smithsonian Institution is so huge that it can only display about 2 percent of its items at all of its museums at any given time. Objects are often rotated, so you may see something your friends didn't when they visited. Even if the items aren't on display, they may be used by scientists and researchers who come from around the world to study the collections.

They're all on the **National Mall.** Many families head to the National Air and Space Museum first. This is a place—like all the other Smithsonian museums—you can come back to again and again and see something different each time!

Look up and you'll find the history of flight hanging above you—the Wright Brothers' airplane, Lindbergh's *Spirit of St. Louis* that he flew to France, the plane Chuck Yeager broke the speed of sound in. Check out the spacecraft! They are so small!

Want to see if you've got the right stuff to be a fighter pilot or an astronaut? Try one of the simulators on the first floor. (There is an extra charge, though.)

Need to rest your tired feet? Even if they're not tired, you'll want to make sure to get tickets for the IMAX Theater that shows movies that have to do with flight and to visit the Albert Einstein Planetarium where you might see the Muppets gang exploring the night sky. (You're never too old for the Muppets!)

If you are visiting on a weekend, check to see if there are any special family programs. Look for the Discovery Stations—movable interactive stations—you'll see around the museum.

You'll definitely want to walk through the Skylab Orbital Workshop (think you'd want to live and work in space for months at a time?) and eat freeze-dried ice cream in the gift shop. You'll find lots of online activities too about space and flight at airandspace.si.edu/education/onlinelearning.cfm.

If you really love space, take time to visit the Steven F. Udvar-Hazy Center near Washington Dulles International Airport—two huge hangars there are filled with rockets, planes, satellites, and more that there isn't room for on the Mall. Come on the second Saturday of each month for Super Science Saturdays (airandspace.si.edu/udvarhazy)!

{ **What's Cool?** The tarantula feedings at the O. Orkin Insect Zoo at the National Museum of Natural History (mnh.si.edu/education/exhibitions/insectzoo.html).

Now imagine what it was like growing up before we had planes and spacecraft. At the National Museum of American History, check out the *America on the Move* exhibit with everything from a Model T Ford (so clunky!) to steam locomotives and even an old-fashioned electric streetcar.

The museum is filled with all sorts of things that Americans have used at home, work, and play—military uniforms, a World War II Jeep, Edison's lightbulb, and Jim Henson's Kermit the Frog and Oscar the Grouch.

By looking closely at this stuff, we can learn a lot about people who lived before us. Check out the website just for kids (americanhistory.si.edu/kids). Pick up a free family guide to hunt for faces of famous figures in American history. Look for hands-on carts and volunteers who can answer your questions.

A VISITING KID SAYS:
"I liked going inside the rocket that spins at the Air and Space Museum."
—Allison, 8, Stuart's Draft, VA

Don't miss the Greensboro Lunch Counter. In 1960, four African-American college students sat down at the lunch counter at Woolworth's in Greensboro, North Carolina, and asked to be served. In many parts of the country at that time, African Americans and other people of color were denied service solely on the basis of race. The students' brave stand against injustice inspired others of all ages to fight for equal rights.

You'll find lots of hands-on activities in the *Price of Freedom: Americans at War* exhibit. Also check out the Star-Spangled Banner (the flag that prompted Francis Scott Key to write the national anthem in 1814) and the sparkling ruby slippers Dorothy wore in the original *Wizard of Oz*.

DID YOU KNOW?

The Smithsonian Institution is so huge that it can only display about 2 percent of its items at all of its museums at any given time. Objects are often rotated, so you may see something your friends didn't when they visited. Even if the items aren't on display, they may be used by scientists and researchers who come from around the world to study the collections.

In the *American Presidency* exhibit, look for the top hat President Lincoln was thought to have worn the night of April 14, 1865, when he was shot at Ford's Theatre. Girls especially like seeing the first ladies' gowns that they wore to the inaugural balls. See how fashion and the role of first ladies have changed through the course of American history.

Not your thing? Maybe you'd rather spend time with dinosaur bones, bugs, and butterflies? Then go to the National Museum of Natural History (on the Mall at 10th Street NW and Constitution Avenue; 202-633-1000; mnh.si.edu).

A VISITING KID SAYS:
"The most interesting thing I saw in Washington, DC was the slave house at the American History Museum."
—Abiah, 9, Virginia Beach, VA

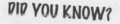

Wow! Look at that giant bull elephant in the rotunda! You can even see the famous Hope Diamond (it's big, more than 45 carats!) here in the Janet Annenberg Hooker Hall of Geology, where you can also walk through a mine and see lots of other gems (check out the 23,000 carat topaz!).

There's a great discovery room just for kids and discovery stations set up throughout the museum, usually in the morning.

Check out the scale model of the real whale scientists call Phoenix and have been tracking for decades—45 feet long!—hanging in the Ocean Hall, where there's also a live coral reef.

DID YOU KNOW?

The cafe at the National Museum of the American Indian has traditional native food from five regions: Northern Woodlands, South America, Northwest Coast, Mesoamerica, and Great Plains. It's called Mitsitam which means "let's eat" in native Piscataway and Delaware languages (nmai.si.edu).

Hate bugs? You can conquer your fear at the O. Orkin Insect Zoo. Want to hold a cockroach?

Maybe ancient creatures are more your thing. At the Dinosaur Hall, you can see skeletons of a stegosaurus and triceratops and fossils from 600 million years ago. In the Discovery Room here, you can touch bones.

Visit in summer and take time for the butterfly pavilion outside with more than two dozen species.

Who says science is boring?

A VISITING KID SAYS:
"My favorite museum was the Natural History Museum because I got to see lots of animals."
—Holden, 13, New Bern, NC

SMITHSONIAN

It all started with a British scientist who never visited the United States. When James Smithson died back in 1829, he left a lot of gold—worth about a half million dollars—to establish an institution to increase knowledge among people. It took until 1846 for Congress to decide to accept the gift. He's buried in the Smithsonian Castle. Today, the Smithsonian includes 19 museums and the National Zoo. Besides the most famous National Air and Space Museum, National Museum of American History, and National Museum of Natural History, you can visit:

- **The Freer Gallery of Art and Arthur M. Sackler Gallery** where you can check out the ImaginAsia weekend workshops for kids and the Enid A. Haupt Garden or listen to stories (asia.si.edu).

- **The Hirshhorn Museum and Sculpture Garden** features guides at special exhibits who can answer questions, and for teens there is a special ArtLab (hirshhorn.si.edu).

What's Cool? The Declaration of Independence, the US Constitution, and the Bill of Rights are housed in a specially sealed case containing the inert gas argon with a controlled amount of humidity to keep the parchment flexible. The case is bulletproof and closely guarded. Every night, the Declaration of Independence, the US Constitution, and the Bill of Rights are lowered into a deep vault down under the Rotunda of the National Archives to keep them safe (archives.gov).

- **The National Museum of African Art** includes cool masks to check out (africa.si.edu)!

- **The National Museum of the American Indian** where you can find a Lakota buffalo headdress and arrowheads (nmai.si.edu).

- **The Renwick Gallery** is the place to see Larry Fuente's *Game Fish* (americanart.si.edu/renwick).

- **The Smithsonian American Art Museum and National Portrait Gallery** is where you'll see the only complete collection of paintings of America's presidents outside the White House as well as portraits of famous sports figures (npg.si.edu).

- **The Anacostia Community Museum** focuses on local African-American art and history and offers free family workshops (anacostia.si.edu).

- **The National Postal Museum** has the largest display of stamps in the United States, planes hanging from the ceiling, and exhibits that let you sort mail (postal museum.si.edu).

DID YOU KNOW?

You can see a 70-million-year-old dinosaur egg at the National Museum of Natural History (mnh.si.edu).

Souvenir Smarts

There are so many options for souvenirs from Washington, DC. Make a plan to be sure you get the one you don't want to leave DC without.

Shop smart! That means talking to your parents about exactly how much you may spend. Save your pennies and quarters before you come. Some families save loose change in a jar to use for vacation souvenirs. Got any birthday money you can add?

Do you want to use your money for one big souvenir (a pricey sweatshirt for your DC football or baseball team)? Or several smaller ones? (How about a Washington Monument to put on your desk?)

Resist those impulse buys and think about choosing something you could only get in Washington, DC. Start a collection! You can buy stickers to put on your reusable water bottle. You can collect pins—as is so popular here—or patches to put on your backpack.

What else could you collect?

The Smithsonian Museums on the National Mall are so big it is wise to take advantage of their websites and print out special family guides before you visit each one. For example, the National Air and Space Museum has one guide, *I Spy in the Sky*, for young children and another, *Looking at Airplanes,* for older children (airandspace.si.edu/visit/guides/selfguides .cfm). There are also special kids gallery guides (airandspace.si.edu/visit/guides/galguides.cfm). Ask for *10 Tips for Visiting Smithsonian Museums with Children,* or you can download the information (si.edu/Content/Pdf/Visit/ SmithsonianKidsTips.pdf). **The Smithsonian experts recommend:**

- Plan ahead to see what special exhibits and programs are available for families by visiting si.edu.

- Wear comfortable shoes. The Smithsonian Museums along the National Mall span an area from 3rd to 14th Street.

- Start your visit at the Smithsonian Information Center in the Castle (1000 Jefferson Dr. SW). It is open daily at 8:30 a.m.—1.5 hours earlier than the museums. This is the place to get all of your questions answered!

- Explore any exhibit that capture's your child's interests even if you hadn't planned to go there.

- Seek out discovery carts and hands-on rooms. Visit the Air and Space Museum's *How Things Fly*, the American History Museum's *The Star-Spangled Banner*, and Postal Museum's *Systems at Work* for hands-on museum fun.

- Continue your Smithsonian adventure afterward at si.edu/kids.

National Archives

How good is your eyesight?

Even with 20-20 vision it's tough to make out the words of the three most important documents in American governmental history at the **National Archives** (7th Street and Constitutional Avenue NW on the Mall; 202-357-5450; archives.gov).

That's because they were written more than two centuries ago!

We're talking about the Declaration of Independence, the US Constitution, and the Bill of Rights—the original

A LOCAL KID SAYS:
"The National Archives is the coolest place to visit in DC because it has lots of history and is the best place to learn interesting facts."
—Catherine, 13, Arlington, VA

documents that set up the US government as a democracy in 1774. If you are visiting on July 4, check out the Patriots in colonial costumes reading the Declaration on the steps.

If you were a member of the Second Continental Congress in 1776, you were a rebel and considered a traitor by the king of England. You knew that a reward had been posted for the capture of certain prominent rebel leaders and signing your name to the Declaration meant that you pledged your life, your fortune, and your sacred honor to the cause of freedom.

Have you seen the movie *National Treasure?* It suggests that something is written on the back of the Declaration of Independence. You can't see the back but it says "Original Declaration of Independence dated 4th July 1776" in reverse. Experts say it is actually ink from the top of the front side that has seeped through the parchment to the back.

A lot of people come to the National Archives to do research. There are tours you can reserve to see how researchers preserve historic documents. You'll find records here of our country's civil, military, and diplomatic activities.

Admission is free, but there can be a long wait. To make an advance reservation, visit recreation.gov.

4

Spies, Tolerance, News,
Money & More—
D Street Now

If you thought museums were

just about art or science, think again.

In Washington, DC there are museums that teach you spy craft and about tolerance, how to fight crime, and the history of the US Navy.

There's a museum about old-fashioned toys, the New Hampshire Toy Attic at the DAR Museum (1776 D St. NW; 202-628-1776; dar.org/museum) and even a museum devoted to architecture and building, The National Building Museum (401 F St. NW; 202-272-2448; nbm.org), where kids like the Amazing Arches activity and a Family Toolkit. There are 50 museums in Washington, DC, so you're bound to find one—or more—that you'd really like to explore.

DID YOU KNOW?

There are special Family Workshops on certain Saturdays during the year where kids can create their own artwork and a special kids' guide to artworks at the Corcoran Gallery of Art, known for its Impressionist and American 19th-century art collections (500 17th St. NW; 202-639-1700; corcoran.org).

Kids are especially drawn to The International Spy Museum (they even have sleepovers here!). You'll find spy games on the website (spymuseum.org/games), and when you visit, you can become a spy in training. You can even see the city as a spy by taking a GPS-guided tour of DC and its neighborhoods. It's your chance to discover the spy capital of the world.

Could you keep your cover? At this museum, you're challenged to adopt a cover identity, memorize specific details about it, and learn firsthand the importance of keeping your "cover." It's not that easy!

What's Cool? You can hear what more than 100 animals sound like at the Mammals Kiosk at the National Geographic Museum where you can learn all about our world and feel a tornado (17th and M Streets NW; 202-857-7588; ngmuseum.org).

Check out what real spies have used—everything from invisible ink to pigeons (a pigeon who carried messages was a decorated World War I vet), buttonhole cameras, bugs of all kinds, and disguise techniques developed by Hollywood for the CIA. The School for Spies gallery has more than 50 years of spy technology developed by agencies from the OSS (the US Office of Strategic Services from World War II) to the KGB (the Russian secret police) and still in use today. Did you know women were spies as far back as the Civil War?

DID YOU KNOW?

There are more than 50 museums in Washington, DC, and 30 of them are free! For a list of museums, visit destinationdc.com.

Older kids also like the National Museum of Crime & Punishment (575 7th St. NW; 202-621-5550; crimemuseum.org) where you can take your place in a lineup or help gather evidence for a crime lab. Look for the special Kid

A LOCAL KID SAYS:
"My favorite museum is the National Museum of Crime & Punishment because it's super big and fun!"
—Safiya, 10, Bowie, MD

Stops where you can see how pirates lived, learn about famous outlaws and the law officers who worked to capture them, see if you can escape from a jail cell, and join in a high-speed chase. Do you think you'd rather be a detective chasing criminals or an investigator chasing forensic clues using science and material evidence?

Of course if you were a reporter, you'd be telling us about the crimes instead of trying to solve them, so head next to The Newseum (555 Pennsylvania Ave. NW; 888-639-7386; newseum.org). If you ever wondered how reporters get the stories that you see online, in newspapers, and on TV, this is the place to come.

Check out the headlines! There are front pages from newspapers all around the world on display each day. Maybe there's one from the town where you're from!

A VISITING KID SAYS:
"My favorite part of the Newseum was the exhibit where you got to act like a newscaster and interact with the camera. I liked it because *SportsCenter* is my favorite show."
—Will, 12, Chicago, IL

The Newseum's 15 major galleries and 15 theaters will immerse you in the world's greatest news stories—from the fall of the Berlin Wall to 9/11. You can see famous photographs that have won the highest honor in photojournalism, the Pulitzer Prize.

Try to imagine what it was like before television and the Internet, when people got their news from newspapers and then radio. Some of the most dramatic events in journalism history are re-created in *I-Witness: A 4-D Time Travel Adventure*. You can play the role of your favorite news anchor at the NBC interactive studio. Everywhere you look there are interactive displays.

Ready to go live on camera?

DID YOU KNOW?

A dollar bill is expected to last less than two years. Workers have shifts all day and all night to print money at the US Bureau of Engraving and Printing. You can watch them work, but it's smart to get tickets ahead of time (14th and C Streets; 866-874-2330; moneyfactory.gov).

Staying Safe on Vacation

In a strange city, especially in a big museum, you can get lost and separated from your parents. The National Museum of Crime & Punishment offers these safety tips:

- Make sure you know how to reach your parents (cell phone number) and the name of the hotel where you are staying and the phone number there.

- Never approach a vehicle, occupied or not, unless you know the owner and are accompanied by a parent, guardian, or other trusted adult.

- Practice "what-if" situations with your parents. What if you got lost? Who would you ask for help?

- During family outings, establish a central, easy-to-locate spot to meet for check-ins or should you get separated.

- Identify those people to ask for help, such as uniformed law enforcement, security guards, and store clerks with nametags.

Treasures to Take Home

When it's time to buy souvenirs, you want to find something you can't get at home. Here's where to go:

Chocolate Moose (1743 L St. NW; 202-463-0992; chocolate moosedc.com) Here's the place to find windup toys, origami dolls, and a great selection of kids' books.

Honest Abe Souvenirs (1000 F St. NW; 202-783-0505 or 202-783-0388; honestabessouvenir.com) One of the largest souvenir shops in DC, Honest Abe has two stories full of DC T-shirts, sports gear from local teams, and personalized license plates from DC.

Labyrinth Games and Puzzles (645 Pennsylvania Ave. SE; 202-544-1059; labyrinthgameshop.com) See what your parents

What's Cool? You can get spy gear for a souvenir at the International Spy Museum (800 F St. NW; 202-393-7798; spymuseum.org).

What's Cool? You can sit at the desk in the "Oval Office" and take a picture with the president and first lady at Madame Tussauds (1001 F St. NW; 202-942-7300; madametussauds.com).

did for fun with nonelectronic puzzles, card games, and board games. Great to play in a hotel room!

National Geographic Store (1145 17th St. NW; events.nationalgeographic.com/events/locations/national-geographic-store) You can find all kinds of maps and treasures from around the world.

Politics and Prose (5015 Connecticut Ave. NW; 202-364-1919; politics-prose.com) Buy a kids' book about your favorite president and see the in-shop printing press.

White House Gifts (701 15th St. NW; 202-737-9500; 1331 Pennsylvania Ave. NW; 202-737-7730; whitehousegifts.com) This shop has two locations; the larger is on 15th Street and has cool souvenirs like presidential bobbleheads and sticker books with the presidents.

Daniel's Story

Imagine if suddenly you had to leave your comfortable home, be separated from your sisters, brothers, and parents, and be sent to a terrible place where you are always hungry and not sure you'll survive.

That's what happened to more than a million children during the Holocaust in Europe during World War II. At the **US Holocaust Memorial Museum** (100 Raoul Wallenberg Place SW; 202-488-0400; ushmm.org), you meet Daniel, who is a composite of many children. You walk through his life—from his comfortable home in Germany to a concentration camp where some of his family died just because they were Jewish. Unfortunately, even today, children and their families are persecuted around the world because of intolerance toward their religion or group. At the museum, you can express how you feel about Daniel's Story and put your message in a museum mailbox.

Experts say you should be 10 to visit the entire US Holocaust Museum. Though Daniel's Story was designed for kids a little younger, it is still very sad. There are memories of those who survived, artwork by children in a concentration camp, and an exhibit about Anne Frank, the young Dutch girl who wrote a diary while in hiding during World War II that we still read today.

It Pays to Be Green

Got a reusable water bottle? All of the plastic from disposable water bottles is really bad for the planet. Using a reusable water bottle is one little thing you can do that can help with this problem in a big way. And your bottle can become a souvenir when you put stickers from your trip to Washington, DC all over it!

Washington, DC has taken a leading role in the green movement. There are 40 miles of bike lanes on city streets and Capital Bikeshare (capitalbikeshare.com), which is a self-service bike rental program that's a first of its kind in the country. Many District hotels have green initiatives to save energy and reduce trash. The Willard InterContinental, for example, is 100 percent powered by wind.

Here are some simple things you can do to help the environment at home and on vacation:

Turn off the lights in your hotel room when you leave.

Recycle.

Reuse towels in the hotel.

Take public transportation when you can.

Take shorter showers.

Carry your water in a reusable water bottle.

TELL THE ADULTS:

Museums can be hard work! Especially when you are touring so many on one trip. Here's how to keep it fun:

- Don't go to a museum when you are tired and/or hungry.

- Wear comfortable shoes.

- Because many museums are too big to explore in one day, take a virtual tour and decide with the whole family what you'd most want to see. Especially in Washington, DC, you'll find special discovery rooms set aside for kids and special family tours and workshops.

- Divide and conquer if there are kids at different ages or having different interests.

- Get some postcards in the museum gift shop when you arrive and have a scavenger hunt as you tour the exhibits.

SECRET CODE

Have you ever created a secret code with your friends? See if you can figure out what silly phrase President Abraham Lincoln said using the code below.

A=X	E=V	I=T	M=L	Q=J	U=H	Y=A
B=Y	F=W	J=O	N=M	R=K	V=C	Z=B
C=Z	G=R	K=P	O=N	S=F	W=D	
D=U	H=S	L=Q	P=I	T=G	X=E	

"PS IUPH PH VJSSXX, KMXYHX ZGPOT NX HJNX IXY; PS IUPH PH IXY, KMXYHX ZGPOT NX HJNX VJSSXX."

"__ ____ __ _____, _____ _____ ____ __ ____ ___;

__ ____ __ ___, _____ _____ __ ____ _____."

See page 152 for the answer!

> Now try and make your own secret message in the space below.

5
The White House

It's a huge mansion

that has 412 doors but no front or back door. The parents who live here have home offices and are always entertaining company. It's also partly your house. In fact, it's called The People's House.

Welcome to the White House, the official residence of the president of the United States and his family (1600 Pennsylvania Ave. NW; 202-456-7041; whitehouse.gov). Did you know that the architect of the White House was chosen in a design competition that received just nine proposals, including one submitted anonymously by Thomas Jefferson?

> ## DID YOU KNOW?
> George Washington never lived in the White House, though he selected the site. John Adams was the first president to live there. He and his wife Abigail moved into the unfinished house in 1800, and every president since has lived there.

The White House is the only building in the world that is the home of a head of state, the executive office of a head of state, and is regularly open to the public for tours. You've probably heard of the West Wing. That's the part of the White House complex where the president and his staff work. Have you seen pictures of the president in the Oval Office?

But if you visit on a public tour—your parents have to get tickets ahead of time from your member of Congress—chances are you won't see the president or any of the first family. If you are very lucky, you might be among the tourists invited out to the South Lawn to watch the president depart or arrive on *Marine One*, the presidential helicopter.

Chances are you really will just see a few of the famous public rooms on your tour. You might see more if you take an interactive tour online (whitehouse.gov/about/inside-white-house/interactive-tour).

DID YOU KNOW?

First children have had pets including ponies, macaws, cats, dogs, snakes, and even raccoons. But dogs have always been the favorite first family pets.

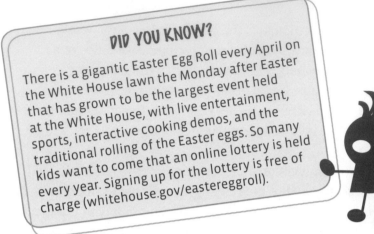
In case you are wondering, there are 132 rooms, 35 bathrooms, 6 levels, and a huge yard of 18 acres filled with fountains, trees, and gardens, many planted by presidents, where the first children and their friends can play. The land around the White House is called President's Park. The president's family has a separate kitchen upstairs in their residence.

Did you know that during the War of 1812, the British set fire to the president's house in 1814? First Lady Dolley Madison famously rescued the portrait of George Washington before she fled the building. The house, of course, was quickly rebuilt, and President James Monroe moved into the new White House in 1817.

Of course you can't touch anything on your tour nor can you turn cartwheels, though that sure would be fun in the big empty East Room where the president and first lady hold big parties. Have you ever been to a party in such a big room? Susan Ford, daughter of President Gerald Ford, had her senior prom there.

Check out the huge dining table in the State Dining Room. It seats as many as 140 guests, and this is where the president and first lady might entertain visiting heads of state.

What's your favorite color? If it's red, green, or blue, you're in luck because you'll be visiting those rooms on your tour—the Red Room, the Green Room, and the Blue Room, where the walls and furniture all match, are all state parlors where the president and first lady might greet guests. Check out the shape of the Blue Room. It's famous for being an oval. Can you count the number of doors in the Red Room? (There are six!)

A VISITING KID SAYS:
"It was cool to see where Obama lives!"
—Arda, 13, Istanbul, Turkey

Like tea? The White House Library has a collection of 2,700 books written by American authors or about American history and is often used for small meetings where they might serve tea.

You probably noticed that the furniture is old and doesn't look very comfortable. But it is very valuable, and some pieces are more than 200 years old.

Enough of this old house? Good thing there's a park right across the street where you can turn all the cartwheels you'd like.

A LOCAL KID SAYS:
"Some locals say that the White House is haunted."
—Riley, 12, Bethesda, MD

DID YOU KNOW?

During World War I, President Woodrow Wilson and First Lady Edith Wilson brought sheep to graze on and fertilize the White House lawns to save on the manpower and money needed to care for them because of the war.

Eating Smart on Vacation

Vacations are a good time to try different foods than just what is on a kids' menu. That's especially true in Washington, DC where you'll find restaurants that feature food from all around the world as well as vegetables and meats from local farmers. Here's how you can eat healthier and try new foods:

Split a portion of something with your brother or sister, your mom or dad.

If there is something you like on the grown-up menu, ask if you can get a half portion or order an appetizer size.

Choose fruit as a snack instead of chips or candy.

Visit a local farmers' market and talk to the farmers.

Drink water rather than a soda.

A VISITING KID SAYS:
"I was surprised by the size of the White House."
—Ebba, 16, Gothenburg, Sweden

White House Vegetable Garden

You can see it from E Street, on the South Lawn of the White House near the tennis courts, and kids just like you—fifth graders from Bancroft Elementary School in Washington— helped get it started.

We're talking about the White House vegetable garden. It's huge—11,100 square feet planted with more than 55 varieties of vegetables, hot peppers, spinach, chard, collards, black kale, berries, and lettuce that are served to famous people who visit the White House as well as to the first family. Another portion of the yields are donated to the local soup kitchen and the Food Bank Organization.

The first White House vegetable garden was planted in 1800, by the second president of the United States John Adams and First Lady Abigail Adams for their family.

The White House vegetable garden that First Lady Michelle Obama started in 2009 with the help of local schoolkids was the first to be planted since World War II, more than 70 years ago, when millions of Victory Gardens sprouted around the country because of food shortages caused by the war. They produced about 40 percent of America's vegetables.

Mrs. Obama, who had no experience in gardening, was motivated to start the garden when she realized her daughters Malia and Sasha were not eating enough healthy meals. The emphasis on the vegetable garden movement is to encourage parents and kids across the country to make healthier food choices.

TELL THE ADULTS:

If you want to visit the White House, you've got to plan ahead—as much as 6 months ahead and no less than 21 days in advance. The experts say don't bring the kids until they are at least 9 or 10.

- You can get a free iPhone app called White House Tour. Visit the iTunes App Store and search for "White House Tour."

- Self-guided tours are available from 7:30 a.m. to 11 a.m. Tuesday through Thursday, 7:30 a.m. to noon Friday, and 7:30 a.m. to 1 p.m. Saturday (excluding federal holidays or unless otherwise noted) and typically last 20 to 35 minutes. They only include the ground and main public floors.

- All White House tours are free of charge, but you need to contact your member of Congress (look them up at house.gov and senate.gov) and request tickets. White House tours may be subject to last-minute cancellation.

- All guests 18 years of age or older will be required to present a valid, government-issued photo identification. All foreign nationals must present their passport. No other forms of foreign identification are accepted.

- All information submitted (e.g., name, date of birth, city, etc.) must exactly match the government-issued photo ID you will present when arriving at the White House.

- You cannot bring items such as cameras and video recorders. If you arrive with them, you won't be able to go inside. Check whitehouse .gov/about/tours-and-events for a full list of what is permitted. You can bring your cell phone, but you aren't permitted to use it. Phones used inside the White House may be confiscated by the US Secret Service.

- All visitors should call the 24-hour Visitors Office information line at (202) 456-7041 to determine if any last-minute changes have been made in the tour schedule.

First Children

Kids have lived in the White House since John Adams brought his three-year-old granddaughter, Susanna, to live there in 1801.

Over the years, some first children have been really little (John Kennedy Jr. was just a baby when he arrived) and in college, like George W. Bush's daughters, Barbara and Jenna. Some had a lot of brothers and sisters (President Theodore Roosevelt had six children who ranged in age from 3 to 16 when their dad was elected), and others, like Chelsea Clinton, had none.

The most recent first kids have been Sasha and Malia Obama. Sasha, who was eight when her father was elected, is the youngest child to reside in the White House since John F. Kennedy Jr. in 1961. (He used to like to hide under his dad's desk in the Oval Office.) Malia Obama was 11 when she moved in.

First children who live in the White House go to school, just like you do, do homework, play on teams, and have friends over to play. Their friends could swim in the pool, golf on the putting green, shoot basketball, go bowling, play tennis, or watch a movie in the theater.

When first children leave the White House, a Secret Service agent travels with them to protect them—whether they are going to school, camp, vacation, or shopping. They are even nearby when they play in the yard or are in their bedroom.

Do you think you'd like to live in the White House?

Find and circle the hidden words!

Democrat	Mansion	Vote
Election	Oval Office	South Lawn
First Lady	President	
Library	Republican	

```
P  W  V  D  R  P  X  W  F  N  O  F  O
R  U  R  E  P  U  B  L  I  C  A  N  V
E  M  W  M  R  O  O  A  R  E  K  A  A
S  A  A  O  L  L  E  B  S  L  B  R  L
I  N  N  C  D  I  V  O  T  E  N  I  O
D  S  D  R  E  B  F  Q  L  R  C  A  F
E  I  B  A  N  R  J  H  A  H  R  O  F
N  O  T  T  L  A  N  O  D  N  H  T  I
T  N  I  P  J  R  C  T  Y  R  R  D  C
B  L  R  M  T  Y  K  O  Z  M  X  T  E
Y  F  S  O  U  T  H  L  A  W  N  V  B
E  L  E  C  T  I  O  N  E  W  Q  P  N
```

See page 153 for the answer!

6

Making Law: US Capitol &
Supreme Court

Wow!

The US Capitol dome is 288 feet high. Check out the painting inside the dome ceiling. It's called the *Apotheosis of Washington,* and it took Italian artist Constantino Brumidi 11 months to finish. *Apotheosis* means the elevation of someone to the rank of a god, so this painting honors George Washington. Did you see the rainbow? It's a symbol of hope.

The **US Capitol** has been Congress's home since 1800. The Senate meets in the area to the north, and the House, to the south. Of course the building has been changed over the years. Take time to look around the famous rotunda. The architecture

A LOCAL KID SAYS:
"The best place to spot celebrities is at the Capitol."
—Brendon, 12, Laurel, MD

is called neoclassical, which was inspired by the style of ancient Greece and Rome, known as classical. Besides the great dome, you'll see columns, a crowning statue, many small windows, repeating small posts, and flat columns. How many can you find?

You'll see lots of works of art throughout the Capitol campus, from bronze and marble statues to oil portraits and murals. Their subjects include prominent Americans, important moments in history, and representations of the nation's ideals—everything from the Embarkation of the Pilgrims to the Declaration of Independence to the Discovery of the Mississippi in the rotunda. Do you have a favorite?

{ **What's Cool?** Getting a flag that has flown over the Capitol. You have to request one through your senator or representative.

A LOCAL KID SAYS:
"Eastern Market, a farmer/flea market, has great deli food and sweet treats."
—Jennie, 11, Bethesda, MD

You'll probably start your visit in the **Capitol Visitor Center** (visit thecapitol.gov) where you can learn about Congress and the Capitol in the huge Exhibition Hall. You can buy souvenirs and even get a snack here.

You can see an exhibit on some of the most important laws Congress has enacted. (Look for the 15th Amendment that gave black men the right to vote.) Check out the 11-foot-high model of the Capitol dome, complete with the *Statue of Freedom* on top. This is one thing you can touch all you like. The US Constitution estab-

lished the three branches of government—the Legislative (Congress), the Executive (led by the president), and

the Judicial (the Supreme Court). (You might visit the US Supreme Court, the highest court of the land, while you are in Washington, DC.)

The Legislative branch—Congress—represents all of us through our representatives and senators. Each state has two senators. Do you know who your representatives and senators are? You can visit their offices at the Capitol.

Congress does more than make laws, though. According to the Constitution, it approves all treaties with other countries, declares all wars, approves presidential nominations, and initiates the removal of federal officials suspected of serious crimes. If you are visiting when Congress is in session, you might be able to watch lawmakers debate from the galleries of the Senate and the House.

A VISITING KID SAYS:
"My favorite part of my visit to Washington, DC was the Duck Tour (dcducks.com). It went for 2 miles on the Potomac River. We even got to help drive the boat!"
—Alexis, 10, Chanhassen, MN

{ **What's Cool?** Visiting the gigantic greenhouse at the US Botanic Garden (100 Maryland Ave. SW; 202-225-8333; usbg.gov). The idea for a national garden dates back to our earliest presidents who wanted to collect and grow plants that would be useful to the American people.

What's Cool? Having lunch at Eastern Market near the Capitol (7th Street and N. Carolina Avenue SE; 202-698-5253; easternmarket-dc.org) where you can sample food from many different countries, buy handmade crafts, and meet local kids. It was built in 1873.

Congress isn't the only place where you might see people debate. If you are lucky, you might be able to hear oral arguments at the US Supreme Court (supremecourt .gov), the highest court in the land. There's a lot of tradition during oral arguments—even where the justices enter (the chief justice and two senior associate justices enter through the center and three junior associate justices

DID YOU KNOW?

Congress is divided into two parts: the House of Representatives and the Senate. Every state has an equal voice in the Senate, while representation in the House of Representatives is based on the size of each state's population.

enter through each side). They sit based on how long they have been on the court, with the chief justice in the middle. Imagine if you always had to sit at dinner based on how old you are!

Often, when the nine justices are debating a controversial issue, you'll see people outside demonstrating about their opinion or side of the issue.

It's a challenge just to get the justices to agree to hear your case. They only review about 100 of more than 10,000 petitions that are filed each term. And no one knows exactly when they will hand down their decisions—just that it will be before the summer recess.

Do you like to argue? Maybe you'd like to argue a case here someday!

A VISITING KID SAYS:
"I enjoyed taking a tour of the Capitol and seeing a lot of statues and old art and taking the underground train from the House to the Senate."
—Jimmy, 10, Bedford, MA

What's Cool? Whispers can be heard from across the room in the Statuary Hall of the Capitol.

Library of Congress

When the British burned the small Library of Congress in 1814, Thomas Jefferson didn't hesitate: He'd spent his whole life collecting books, and he offered them as a replacement.

His library was considered one of the best libraries in the country, and his 6,487 books became the foundation for the new Library of Congress.

Today the **Library of Congress** (10 1st St. SE across from the Capitol; 202-707-8000; americaslibrary .gov) in the Thomas Jefferson Building has more than 144 million items including 34.5 million books in 460 languages, and the largest rare book collection in North America. The library also has films, maps, music, and sound recordings. The library occupies three buildings.

Need homework help? Ask a librarian a question online (loc.gov/rr/askalib). There is also a kids' section on the website (loc.gov/families).

There's also a Young Readers Center where you can browse books yourself, and the Library of Congress

Experience uses technology to give you amazing access. You can turn the pages of books from Jefferson's library, examine pages from the Gutenberg Bible (printed way back in 1455!), and even investigate edits made in the rough draft of the Declaration of Independence and play Knowledge Quest, an interactive game of discovery.

Take a guided tour or look around yourself. There are special tours if you love music, history, books, and, of course, Thomas Jefferson. Make sure to take a look at the Great Hall and the Gutenberg Bible and the Giant Bible of Mainz.

DID YOU KNOW?

E Pluribus Unum is Latin for "Out of Many, One." You'll see those words on the Great Seal of the United States that was first used in 1782 and is still used today.

The dome of the US Capitol weighs 9 million pounds.

The Library of Congress is the world's largest library.

A Language All Their Own

Words have entirely different meanings in political circles here in Washington, DC.

SPIN: what politicians say to members of the media to explain their point of view

PORK BARREL: when elected officials add funding for their special projects to a bill that has no relation to that project

GATE: any kind of scandal (the term started with the famous Watergate scandal in the 1970s)

STUMP: what politicians do when they are campaigning

LOBBY: what someone does when he or she wants to convince a lawmaker to support a particular agenda

BILL: what a proposed law is called

A VISITING KID SAYS:
"I learned that the White House, Supreme Court, and Congress are separate branches of government."
—Ebba, 16, Gothenburg, Sweden

Capitol Etiquette

The Capitol is a working office building full of very valuable and historic sculptures, paintings, and more. As at other historic sites in Washington, DC, you need to be respectful when you visit. Here's how:

Turn off and do not use your cell phone or other electronic devices during the orientation film and while touring the Capitol.

Use your quiet voice when walking through the Capitol and exploring the Capitol Visitor Center's Exhibition Hall.

Do not touch art objects including sculptures, statues, walls, and cases. The oils and acids on even clean hands can cause damage to works of art that cannot be corrected.

Don't lean on the walls or sit on displays or sculptures.

Respect any areas that are roped off.

Don't run, push, shove, or do anything that may endanger other visitors or the works of art and the items in the Exhibition Hall.

DID YOU KNOW?

The huge Statue of Freedom on top of the Capitol is holding a sword (a symbol of war) and a shield (a symbol of protection). She's also holding a wreath of laurel leaves (representing peace).

TELL THE ADULTS:

You must book tickets in advance to enter the Capitol (tours.visitthecapitol.gov). For a smaller tour that might focus more on your state, you can book through your senator or representative's office (you can find your representative at house.gov and senator at senate.gov or call 202-225-6827). Tours of the historic US Capitol are free; however, tour passes are required. The Capitol is open Monday through Saturday, 8:30 a.m. to 4:30 p.m. Tours of the Capitol begin with a 13-minute orientation film and last approximately one hour. If you haven't gotten passes in advance, it still may be worth a call or stop at your representatives' office to see if they can help you.

If Congress is in session and you want to watch in the House or Senate gallery, you must stop at your senator or representative's office first and get a pass. To find out when Congress is meeting, go to house.gov or senate.gov. As when you visit the White House, you can't go inside if you have any aerosol or nonaerosol sprays, cans, bottles, oversize suitcases, duffels, or large backpacks. Food and beverages (including water bottles) are prohibited in the building.

Especially when touring with younger kids, it is smart to explain the significance of visiting the Capitol first. Use an example of a law that affects them—car seats and seat belts in cars, for example. There is a special kids' guide that you can download (visitthecapitol.gov/education/my_capitol student_self_guide).

There are also special family tours of the Library of Congress certain times of the year and others that talk about music and the performing arts and Thomas Jefferson. Check loc.gov/visit/tours/guided for details and download a Virtual Tour for your iPhone. Free lectures about the US Supreme Court (supremecourt.gov) are offered daily. To see the Court in session, you need to plan your trip to match the court's schedule: Cases are heard Monday through Wednesday from October through April. Be forewarned that children must be able to sit quietly and sometimes lines start forming before the building even opens. Seating is first-come, first-served. If you want to just watch briefly, get in the three-minute line.

The Pentagon

Welcome to the **Pentagon**, headquarters of the Army, Navy, Air Force, Marines, and Coast Guard (pentagon.afis.osd .mil). It's not actually in Washington, DC but across the 14th Street Bridge in Arlington, Virginia. The Pentagon is a five-side building, which is how it got its name! It is the world's largest office building, and some 23,000 people work there. There are around 18 miles of hallways!

You can take a public tour, but be prepared to walk a lot—you'll cover more than a mile! If you visit, make sure to go to Pentagon Memorial Park where you can see 184 benches, one for each victim of the terrorist attacks on September 11, 2001. The 59 benches facing the Pentagon are for those who died inside, and the 125 facing the opposite direction are for the passengers who died on American Airlines Flight 77 that crashed into the building.

MAKING LAWS

Draw a line representing a law from the Capitol to the president's desk.

7
Music, Plays & More

If you thought Washington, DC

was just about historic monuments, museums, and government, think again.

It's also about music, theater, puppet shows, dance, and lots of performances that are designed especially for kids.

What's your favorite?

Do you play an instrument? You might want to see a DC Youth Orchestra performance (dcyop.org) or the musicians at the Kennedy Center. Go at 6 p.m. for a free concert at the **Millennium Stage** (2700 F St. NW; 800-444-1324; kennedy-center.org) or to one of their **Kinderkonzerts.** Check the Kennedy Center website for the schedule of programs for Young Audiences. In summer, you can watch them perform outdoors at Wolf Trap Farm Park for the Performing Arts where there's also **Children's Theatre-in-the-Woods** (1551 Trap Rd., Vienna, VA; 703-255-1868; wolftrap.org).

DID YOU KNOW?

Local kids have created podcasts especially for visiting kids, with the help of Destination DC (destinationdc.com). Check them out at washington.org/visiting/experience-dc/family/podcasts-for-kids.

Presidents and their families go to performances. So do local families (it's a tradition to see Dickens's Christmas Carol at Ford's Theatre, 511 10th St. NW; 202-347-4833; fords theatre.org) and visiting families like yours. It will be a nice change of pace from all the sightseeing you've been doing. Just make sure you're not too tired or hungry when you go to see a play or musical performance.

Sometimes you have to get tickets in advance, but other times you can just decide to go that day. There are a lot of free performances too. There's entertainment some afternoons at The Old Post Office Pavilion, where you can also get lunch and shop (1100 Pennsylvania Ave. NW; 202-289-4224; oldpostofficedc .com). In summer there are free lunchtime concerts at the Ronald Reagan Building called Live! On Woodrow Wilson Plaza (13th Street and Pennsylvania Avenue NW; 202-312-1300; itcdc .com). Check out Imagination Stage where musicals aren't too long, and if you are lucky, you can sit on a cushion right near the stage (4908 Auburn Ave., Bethesda, MD; 301-280-1660; imaginationstage.org).

The Children's Theater has been around for more than four decades! It's nearby in Arlington, Virginia, at the Thomas Jefferson Community Theatre (125 Old Glebe Rd; 703-548-1154; encorestage.org).

The Kennedy Center has special Performances for Young Audiences—everything from concerts to storytelling.

DID YOU KNOW?

The Kennedy Center is a living memorial to President John F. Kennedy who had taken the lead in raising money for the National Cultural Center. Today the Kennedy is home to the National Symphony Orchestra, the Washington National Opera, and the Suzanne Farrell Ballet, and you will see all kinds of performances here (2700 F St. NW; 202-416-8000; kennedy-center.org).

Maybe you'll be in town for a special Saturday workshop at the Folger Theatre. If you are visiting around Shakespeare's birthday (held on the Sunday closest to April 23), don't miss the bash with jugglers, crafts, and, of course, birthday cake (folger.edu)!

If you like politics, you'll like the Capitol Steps, the musical political satire troupe of former congressional staffers turned comedians and songwriters. They perform every Friday and Saturday night at the Ronald Reagan Building Amphitheater (1300 Pennsylvania Ave. NW; 202-312-1300; capsteps.com).

If you dance, you'll like the Washington Ballet, which performs at the Kennedy Center. You can see ethnic dance performances at Dance Place, including a weeklong Dance Africa Festival, a Tap Dance Festival, and free summer events (3225 8th St. NE; 202-269-1600; danceplace.org). If you sing in a chorus, you'll love the Fairfax Choral Society with both kids and adults in suburban Virginia (4028 Hummer Rd., Annandale, VA; 703-642-3277; fairfaxchoral society.org).

What's your pick? Now you just have to convince the rest of your family to come along!

A VISITING KID SAYS:
"I didn't see any performances at a theater in Washington, DC, but I did get to see some people singing on the street!"
—Daniel, 10, Henderson, SC

What's Cool? The free National Symphony Orchestra concerts on Memorial Day weekend, Fourth of July, and Labor Day at the US Capitol.

Bells, Trumpets & Soldiers

They're free and they're fun. We're talking about **military band concerts.** Check online to see if one is scheduled during your visit (usarmyband.com).

Marine Corps Friday Evening—dress parades all summer. You need reservations for these. Get them online at barracks .marines.mil. They are held at the US Marine Barracks, 8th and 1st Streets SE. Netherlands Carillon Concerts take place at the Marine Corps War Memorial near Arlington National Cemetery (nps.gov/gwmp/nethcarillon.htm).

At the **Sunset Parade at the Marine Corps War Memorial** you can hear the Marine Drum and Bugle Corps and see drills certain evenings in summer (drumcorps.mbw.usmc.mil).

Ford's Theatre

When Abraham Lincoln was president, Ford's Theatre was a popular stage for plays and musical productions. On April 14, 1865, President Lincoln visited Ford's for his 12th time. At this performance, Lincoln was shot by John Wilkes Booth, a young theater star who had performed at Ford's Theatre. Lincoln died the next morning in the Petersen House, a boarding-house located across the street. **Ford's Theatre** (511 10th St. NW; 202-347-4833; fordstheatre.org) remained closed for more than 100 years. It reopened in 1968 as a national historic site and working theater (you might be able to see a

A VISITING KID SAYS:
"I enjoyed seeing the old artifacts at Ford's Theatre and hearing the sad story about how Lincoln died. I learned that John Wilkes Booth made it public that he shot Lincoln."
—Rachel, 9, Rosendale, WI

play here). It is operated through a public-private partnership between Ford's Theatre Society and the National Park Service. Today, the museum tells the story of Abraham Lincoln's presidency, from his arrival in Washington in 1861 to the legacy he left. The exhibits also paint a picture of Washington, DC and the United States during Lincoln's presidency. The Ford's Center for Education and Leadership, which is located at 514 10th St. NW, across the street from the theater and adjacent to the Petersen House, where Lincoln died, will tell you more about Lincoln's legacy. There's even a re-creation of the Virginia tobacco barn where John Wilkes Booth was ultimately captured and killed. Today you can learn about the day Lincoln died during special theatrical performances and hear talks by National Park Service rangers. At the museum, you can see what it was like to live in Civil War—era Washington. You can even take a special History on Foot walking tour led by an actor dressed as a Civil War character.

TELL THE ADULTS:

There are many opportunities in Washington, DC to introduce kids to theater and musical productions, without spending a lot of money. Military band concerts are free. Find half-priced tickets to many events at TICKETplace (407 7th St. NW; 202-842-5387; ticketplace.org) the day of the performance. At Arena Stage, half-price HotTix tickets go on sale at the box office 30 minutes before curtain. Students get 35 percent off; purchase by phone or in person (1101 6th St. SW; 202-488-3300; arenastage.org).

- For the National Theatre's free performance series "Saturday Morning at the National Theatre," tickets are distributed on a first-come, first-served basis 30 minutes before the curtain goes up (1321 Pennsylvania Ave. NW; 202-628-6161; nationaltheatre.org). The daily free performances at the Kennedy Center Grand Foyer are at 6 p.m. (2700 F St. NW; 800-444-1324; kennedy-center.org).

- Pay what you like for the first performances of every main stage series at the Woolly Mammoth Theatre (641 D St. NW; 202-289-2443; woolly-mammoth.net).

- The Washington Ballet's "beerandballet&bubbly" program lets you go to the ballet school to watch an open rehearsal and mingle with dancers afterward. Each preview is $25 and usually runs before a major performance; call (202) 362-3606. Check out the latest performance at the Smithsonian's family-friendly Discovery Theater. Shows range from tap dance performances to puppet show workshops, and tickets are always under $10 for kids (1100 Jefferson St. SW; 202-633-8700; discoverytheater.org).

- Free, live jazz at the Smithsonian American Art Museum's "Take Five!" performance series usually happens on the third Thursday of each month, and the museum's cafe stays open so guests can enjoy beverages and light snacks during the performance (8th and F Streets NW; 202-633-7970; americanart.si.edu/calendar/performances/music/five). At George Washington University's Lisner Auditorium (730 21st St. NW; 202-994-6800; lisner.org), free shows are sprinkled throughout the performance calendar year-round.

Just Desserts

Especially after you've seen a concert or a play, it's fun to go out for dessert. And Washington, DC has plenty of choices:

Dolcezza Artisanal Gelato (1560 Wisconsin Ave. NW; 202-333-4646; dolcezzagelato.com) Located in Georgetown, Dolcezza's gelato is made with local ingredients that come from orchards and farms around the DC area.

Georgetown Cupcake (3301 M St. NW; 202-333-8448; georgetowncupcake.com) You might have seen the two "cupcake sisters" on TV. Their shop has more than 100 flavors to choose from.

Pleasant Pops (202-596-8440; pleasantpops.com) The place for popsicles all made with seasonal ingredients (think Pineapple Basil and Summer Strawberry). Look for them at farmers' markets and other events. Check out their website for locations.

Sticky Fingers Treats and Eats (1370 Park Rd. NW; 202-299-9700; stickyfingersbakery.com) If you've got allergies, the Sticky Fingers bakers churn out an array of vegan, and often nut-free and gluten-free, sweets.

Sugar Magnolia (3417 Connecticut Ave. NW; 202-244-7995; rippledc.com) Sugar Magnolia in the Cleveland Park neighborhood near the National Zoo is known for their yummy ice cream sandwiches—including weird flavors like maple bacon.

{ **What's Cool?** Hanging out at the National Harbor along the Potomac where you can shop, eat, and in summer, watch free movies outside on Sunday (nationalharbor.com).

8

National Zoo

Lions and tigers and pandas!

No matter when you visit, something is always happening at the National Zoo. You might be able to watch the staff feed spiders or help feed fish at the Kids' Farm where you can also learn about farming, meet a Great Cats keeper, or even watch an octopus have a meal. Check the daily program schedule when you arrive.

Did you know you can travel halfway around the world without leaving Washington, DC? Welcome to the Asia Trail where there are species native to Asia including the zoo's most popular residents, the giant pandas, of course. Don't miss the flamingos, toucans, and kiwi at the Bird House. There are hundreds of birds here from all over the globe. But those aren't all the birds at this zoo: More than 159 wild bird species live in the trees and park around the zoo.

DID YOU KNOW?

Asian elephants weigh up to 11,000 pounds. They are endangered, and their population has declined by 70 percent. To protect the future of Asian elephants, the National Zoo has launched a campaign to save them by breeding and helping scientists care for them.

A VISITING KID SAYS:
"My favorite part of the zoo was seeing the otters. They are enjoyable to watch."
—Jacob, 12, Stuart's Draft, VA

You've got to stop at the Great Ape House. The gorillas live in family groups just like you do. You can see monkeys in the Small Mammal House. Stop in at the Reptile Discovery Center and meet snakes that live in the desert. Have you ever seen a Sumatran tiger? You will at Great Cats! Here you'll also learn that it's the female lions that go out and hunt as a group while the males stay behind and protect the territory. Lions are very social, but tigers tend to hunt and live alone, except when they are breeding or a female has cubs.

At the Kids' Farm, you can help groom the animals in the Caring Corral and, in the Barn, learn all about alpacas,

What's Cool? Watching the giant pandas play with the special toys the keepers have prepared for them with treats inside.

cows, donkeys, hogs, and goats. Check out the Pizza Garden to find out how pizza ingredients are grown and play in the Giant Pizza Playground. Have you ever gotten up close and personal with a goat? You can at the Kids' Farm! Wow, there's so much to do at the National Zoo.

Those who run the zoo say you definitely want to:

- Watch the giant pandas in the Giant Panda Habitat.

- Meet the gorillas in the Great Ape House.

- See the Asian elephants.

- Laugh at the orangutans as they cross the famous O Line.

- Step into the Bird House's Indoor Flight Room and watch as parrots, tanagers, and many other bird species fly freely.

> **DID YOU KNOW?**
> The pandas each eat 50 pounds of bamboo a day as well as nutritious biscuits, carrots, and apples. The bamboo is grown on a farm in Maryland.

- View the African lion pride—including young lions—and Sumatran tigers at Great Cats.

- See the giant Pacific octopus and other creatures in the invertebrate exhibit.

- Walk through the rain forest in the Amazonia exhibit as monkeys leap and birds fly around you.

- Unearth the secret life of naked mole rats in the Small Mammal House.

Panda Power

Mei Xiang (her name means "beautiful fragrance" in Chinese) and Tian Tian (his name means "more and more") are the National Zoo's giant pandas, on a 10-year loan from China as part of a research, conservation, and breeding program.

It can be hard to tell them apart. Tian Tian has black knee socks and two black dots across the bridge of his nose. Mei Xiang has black high-stockings up her hind legs and a pale black band across her nose.

Mei Xiang gave birth to a male cub, Tai Shan ("peaceful mountain"), on July 9, 2005. He has moved back to China.

The pandas live at the Fujifilm Giant Panda Habitat, a state-of-the-art indoor and outdoor exhibit designed to mimic the pandas' natural habitat of rocky, lush terrain in China. Ever since the National Zoo received Hsing-Hsing and Ling-Ling from China in 1972 as part of President Richard Nixon's historic visit, scientists at the National Zoo have been leaders in studying pandas and saving them in the wild. Giant pandas are endangered. There are only about 1,600 left in the wild.

At the zoo, the Fujifilm Giant Panda Habitat is the gateway to the Asia Trail; the six other species living along the trail are sloth bears, fishing cats, clouded leopards, red pandas, Asian small-clawed otters, and a Japanese giant salamander.

Endangered Species and How You Can Help

An *endangered species* is an animal or plant that is in danger of disappearing completely from our planet. Nearly a quarter of the National Zoo is made up of endangered species, and these include giant pandas, Asian elephants, white-naped cranes, and western lowland gorillas.

Many other species are threatened, which means that unless conservation efforts are started, they're likely to become endangered.

Many animals at the National Zoo are part of conservation efforts, and the 3,200-acre campus of the Smithsonian Conservation Biology Institute in Virginia oversees the Smithsonian's effort to understand and protect species. Animals and humans are part of one world with one ocean; it is up to us to protect it. You can adopt a species at the National Zoo to help support the care of the animals (nationalzoo.si .edu), and there is a special Kids' Area on the National Zoo website that will tell you more about Giant Pandas and conservation efforts. But every day you can do small, simple things to help the planet, such as:

Turn off lights when you leave a room. Turn off the television if no one is watching it.

Create a recycling center in your home and recycle newspapers, glass, and aluminum cans.

Turn off the water while brushing your teeth.

Use both sides of a piece of paper.

Plant wildflowers in your garden instead of picking them from the wild.

Reduce the amount of trash you create: Reuse your lunch bag each day.

Don't buy animals or plants taken illegally from the wild or that are not native to your area. Ask where they're from.

Share what you know with family and friends.

TELL THE ADULTS:

Go early to the zoo and take public transportation if you can. Parking is limited, and some days in spring and summer, lots are filled by midmorning. Print out the Zoo Crew Training Manual Family Guide with activities you can share as you visit. Customize your zoo experience with the National Zoo's first app for mobile devices, now available for purchase from the App Store and Google Play for $1.99, which includes the zoo's most popular webcams of the animals.

To enhance your visit, you can sign on for an immersion tour or one especially geared for kids:

- The National Zoo has a behind-the-scenes tour at Elephant Trails with a personal guide, which includes the state-of-the-art barn that isn't usually open to visitors and the chance to see the keepers at work (nationalzoo.si.edu/Animals/AsianElephants/ElephantTrails/tour.cfm).

- There is Snore & Roar, the chance to sleep over with your favorite animals (great apes, great cats, or elephants, for example), get a special tour with the keeper, and take a flashlight hike through the zoo to check out the nocturnal animals. You must join FONZ, Friends of the National Zoo, to participate (nationalzoo.si.edu/activitiesandevents/activities/snoreroar).

- The National Aquarium, Baltimore, offers dolphin encounters, training sessions with the dolphins, and sleepovers with the sharks and dolphins, among other activities (aqua.org/explore/baltimore/immersion-tours).

- Check out gosmithsonian.com for a list of the latest Smithsonian activities.

- Washington Walks (202-484-1565; washington walks.com) has special themed tours including "In Fala's Footsteps" for kids (Fala was FDR's dog) and private tours that can focus on your kids' interests.

DID YOU KNOW?

The National Aquarium in Washington, DC is the oldest aquarium in the country (in the basement of the Department of Commerce building on 14th Street NW at Constitution Avenue; 202-482-2826; nationalaquarium.org).

The National Aquarium

Birds, amphibians, reptiles, marine mammals, and more . . . more than 16,000, that is! Welcome to the **National Aquarium** (501 East Pratt St., Baltimore, MD; 410-576-3800; aqua .org), right in downtown Baltimore's Inner Harbor and on the shores of Chesapeake Bay. (The much smaller National Aquarium, Washington, DC, is located in the Commerce Building, 14th and Constitution Avenue NW; 202-482-2825.)

If you love aquariums, you'll love the National Aquarium, Baltimore. The main building holds 1 million gallons of water! You can travel from the top of the rain forest to the bottom of the ocean; check out all kinds of sharks. See one of the biggest stingray collections in the country, watch a 4-D movie, and explore Maryland's diverse sea life and an Atlantic coral reef with more than 500 exotic fish. Have you ever seen a porcupine fish?

This isn't only a place to see sea creatures, though. From the Chesapeake Bay to Costa Rica, the National Aquarium programs help people apply solutions for protecting marine life and coastlines. The aquarium helps rescue and rehabilitate stranded animals in the Chesapeake Bay. You can learn about these efforts when you visit. Everyone loves the dolphins. Aren't they funny?

NATIONAL ZOO ANIMAL SCAVENGER HUNT

Check off the animals you see!

- ❏ A donkey
- ❏ A flamingo
- ❏ A gorilla
- ❏ A lemur
- ❏ A lion
- ❏ A mole rat
- ❏ A panda
- ❏ A tiger
- ❏ A wallaby
- ❏ A zebra

DID YOU KNOW?

The National Zoo was one of the first zoos to establish a scientific research program. Today, the zoo's research team studies animals both in the wild and at the zoo.

9

Get Outdoors!

Got your Frisbee?

Maybe you'd rather have a soccer ball or softball. It doesn't matter what you bring as long as you've got shoes on you can jump or run in.

Museums are great, but tell your parents there's plenty to see outdoors in Washington, DC—on foot, in kayaks, and on bikes.

Local kids especially like **Rock Creek Park,** the biggest by far of Washington parks. It's 4 miles long and one of the oldest and largest urban parks in the entire national park system! You can become a junior ranger at Rock Creek Park and get the activity book online. There's a Nature Center with a hands-on discovery room and planetarium.

A LOCAL KID SAYS:
"The coolest place to visit in Washington, DC is the Rock Creek Park Nature Center. It's fun, and you can learn interesting facts there."
—Tate, 11, Washington, DC

Watch the bees in their hive, take a guided nature walk with a ranger, or head out with your family from the Nature Center. Maybe you can help feed the Nature Center's creatures (5200 Glover Rd. NW; 202-426-6829; nps.gov/rocr)!

Like stars? There's a special stargazing one Saturday a month at the planetarium from April through November. Call the Nature Center at (202) 895-6070 or check the Internet sites nps.gov/rocr/planyourvisit/planetarium.htm or capitalastronomers.org for the schedule. Take a hike at the Edge of the Woods Trail and see how many different trees you can find. Remember not to take anything home from the park, though. How many animals do you see? There's everything from wood ducks to gray foxes to raccoons, squirrels, deer, and even painted turtles here.

Visit Peirce Barn to learn more about milling along the creek and how mills at one time used the creek for power. Stop at the Old Stone House in Georgetown and look at all the things from colonial times—including children's toys. The Old Stone House is one of the oldest buildings in Washington, DC, and the rangers protect it so we can learn what life was like for families in the early days of our nation.

You can also go horseback riding (rockcreekhorsecenter .com), play golf, go on a long bike ride through the park, or have a picnic.

You can rent bikes at places like **Bike and Roll** (202-842-BIKE; bikeandroll.com) that also offer guided bike rides.

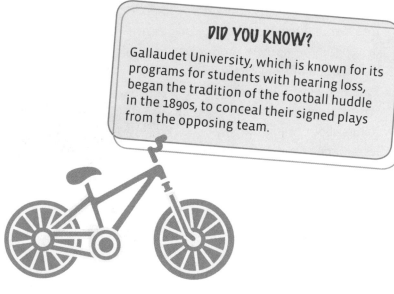

DID YOU KNOW?

Gallaudet University, which is known for its programs for students with hearing loss, began the tradition of the football huddle in the 1890s, to conceal their signed plays from the opposing team.

Maybe you'd rather be on the water. Check out **DC Ducks,** a tour that uses vehicles that can travel on land and in the water (855-323-8257; dcducks.com).

> A VISITING KID SAYS:
> "I liked that there are a lot of trees in the city."
> —Louis, 12, Glendale, CA

The Chesapeake and Ohio Canal runs 185 miles and was originally built to connect tidewater on the Potomac River with the Ohio River in Pennsylvania for a shipping lane. During the years following the Civil War, 850,000 tons of coal were carried down the canal!

What's Cool? Playing at Friendship Park (aka Turtle Park), DC's most popular playground, located in the city's American University Park neighborhood.

Today besides kayaking and canoeing, families like to hike and bike here. Like flowers? Visit the National Arboretum (3501 New York Ave. NE; 202-245-2726; usna.usda.gov). Buy some food and feed the fish in the pond. Some are huge! See how many herbs you recognize in the Herb Garden and don't miss the National Bonsai Collection. Some have been growing here for hundreds of years. There is even a Youth Garden that local kids have helped plant. Maybe you'll get some ideas for your garden at home!

DC for Free!

There's a lot to choose from in Washington, DC that won't cost anything, or just a few dollars, especially outside:

See the National Mall with DC by Foot (freetoursbyfoot .com/dc), a walking tour company that gives free, kid-friendly tours (gratuity recommended) with games and fun facts. Tours include Arlington National Cemetery, the Lincoln Assassination, the Twilight Tour, and free bus tours.

Head to East Potomac Golf Course for a round of minia-ture golf. Players 18 and under pay $5 per game. Check out the views of the river and planes landing at Reagan National Airport (golfdc.com).

Fly a kite next to the Washington Monument for a great family photo.

See the stars in Rock Creek Park at the only planetarium operated by the National Park Service. Tours of the night sky are free (nps.gov/rocr/planyourvisit/planetarium.htm).

Start a game of Frisbee on the National Mall, or a game of volleyball at one of the pits at Potomac Park.

Walk in the footsteps of a great thinker and advocate for freeing slaves at Cedar Hill, formerly the private home of Frederick Douglass. While there, take in great views of the city across the Anacostia River. Tours are free with a small booking fee (nps.gov/frdo).

Play Ball!

Take your pick—baseball, soccer, football, hockey, or basketball. . . . No matter when you visit, you can probably go watch your favorite sport:

DC United, men's soccer, from early April to mid-October (RFK Stadium, 2400 E. Capitol St. SE; 292-587-5000; dcunited.com)

Washington Capitals, hockey, from early October to April (Verizon Center, 601 F St. NW; 202-628-3200; capstickets.net)

Washington Freedom, women's soccer, from early April to mid-August (18031 Central Park Circle, Boyds, MD; 202-547-5425; washingtonfreedom.com)

A LOCAL KID SAYS:
"The DC Capitals games are intense!"
—Riley, 12, Bethesda, MD

Washington Nationals, baseball, from early April to late September (1500 S. Capitol St. SE; 202-675-6287; nationals.mlb.com)

Washington Redskins, football, from early September to late December (FedEx Field, 1600 FedEx Way, Landover, MD; 301-276-6000; redskins.com)

Washington Wizards, basketball, from November to April (Verizon Center, 601 F St. NW; 202-628-3200; nba.com/wizards)

Locals also root for Baltimore teams—the **Baltimore Orioles** baseball team (333 W. Camden St., Baltimore, MD; 888-848-2473; orioles.mlb.com—Camden Yards is a really cool ballpark!) and the **Baltimore Ravens** football team (M&T Bank Stadium, 1101 Russell St., Baltimore, MD; 410-261-7283; baltimoreravens.com).

Festival Fever

Like kites?

If you're lucky, you'll be in Washington, DC during a festival. Kids especially like the Blossom Kite Festival, which is part of the National Cherry Blossom Festival in April, a festival that draws kite makers from all over the country. There are prizes for homemade kites too.

The **National Cherry Blossom Festival,** of course, is when thousands of cherry trees bloom in April. There are parades, free concerts, fireworks, and more (nationalcherry blossomfestival.org). Kids also love the **Festival of American Folklife** in July, a 10-day festival on the National Mall with lots of music, crafts, and good eats (festival.si.edu).

If you're in Washington, DC for the holidays, don't miss the **Holiday Celebration at the National Museum of American History** (si.edu).

Bring a blanket to the National Mall to watch outdoor films on a gigantic screen during **Screen on the Green** in July and August (friendsofscreenonthegreen.org).

GET OUTDOORS DECODER

Where is one of DC's most beautiful locations (and we mentioned it earlier in this chapter)? Find the missing letters in these other DC-related words and fill in the letter next to the matching number find out what the letters spell!

1. F__iendship
2. Bl__ssoms
3. Ana__ostia
4. Reds__ins
5. __edar Hill
6. F__eedom
7. Unit__d
8   Pr__sident
9. Nationals Par__
10. Ca__itols
11. Potom__c
12. Wiza__ds
13. American University Par__

{ **What's Cool?** Canoeing or kayaking on the Potomac. There are boathouses along the Georgetown waterfront where you can rent canoes and kayaks by the hour. Try Fletcher's Boat House (4940 Canal Rd. NW; 202-244-0461; fletchersboat house.com) where you can also get a fishing license.

__ __ __ __   __ __ __ __ __   __ __ __ __
1 2 3 4   5 6 7 8 9   10 11 12 13

See page 153 for the answer!

10

George Washington,
Thomas Jefferson,
the Revolutionary War
& More

His education stopped

when he was 14. By the time he was 17, he was working on the frontier. He almost died when he fell out of a raft into icy water!

And that was just the beginning of George Washington's life and adventures. He was, of course, the commander of the Continental Army during the Revolutionary War. In one of his finest moments, he resigned his commission in 1783, giving up power and returning to his home in Mount Vernon. He famously refused to be named king. He thought he was done with public service and politics.

{ **What's Cool?** Taking a riverboat down the Potomac from Washington, DC to Mount Vernon from March through October (205-554-8000; cruisetomountvernon.com).

But lucky for us, he was wrong. Washington was elected the first president of the United States, and he shaped the role of the president. He appointed the first cabinet and designated the site for the nation's new capital. Washington refused a third term and retired in 1797. He died just two years later and is buried at Mount Vernon, just 16 miles south of Washington, DC on the banks of the Potomac River. You can visit Washington's Tomb here. Over a million people come to the site each year.

A VISITING KID SAYS:
"I enjoyed driving around the Civil War battlefields and seeing the memorials. I learned a lot about Lincoln!"
—Grant, 11, Northfield, MN

Farther south in Virginia, about two and half hours from Washington, DC on a hilltop outside Charlottesville, you can visit **Monticello,** Thomas Jefferson's home and plantation (monticello.org). Jefferson was also the founder of the University of Virginia, which is in Charlottesville. Don't miss the hands-on activity center if you visit. Have you ever written with a quill pen?

Many families include **Mount Vernon** when they are visiting Washington, DC because it is so close. There's a lot to do—and to learn—when you visit Mount Vernon. You probably want to start in the Ford Orientation Center with the adventure movie that will explain key moments in Washington's life and in American history. Check out the tiny Mount Vernon in Miniature while you are there—all 22 rooms! Make sure to pick up an Adventure Map so you can solve the puzzles as you walk around. You might even be able to earn a scout badge during your visit.

A LOCAL KID SAYS:
"At Monticello, the most interesting part was the tour about the experiences of enslaved people."
—William, 12, Potomac, MD

Did you know George Washington had false teeth? You can see them at the Donald W. Reynolds Museum and Education Center along with his shoe buckle, his old-style pants known as breeches, dictionaries, maps, and more.

Your parents will want to tour George Washington's mansion. Look for clues to Washington's likes and even his aspirations for the fledgling United States. See the swivel chair he used during his presidency. Imagine what it must have been like to live here in the summer before air-conditioning.

DID YOU KNOW?

George Washington probably never chopped down a cherry tree. A man who wrote a biography of George Washington shortly after he died invented the story.

George Washington made provisions in his will to free all the slaves that belonged to him.

You'll probably have more fun out and about. Check out the sunken fences called ha-ha walls built into the hillside. They were designed to keep the animals from getting too close to the house, but you couldn't see them from the house or the lawns.

Look for costumed interpreters circulating every day to tell you what it was like to live at Mount Vernon during George Washington's time. You can even meet Martha Washington! There are special tours led by people from Washington's world, including his granddaughter, as they go about their daily activities.

DID YOU KNOW?

Besides being a statesman and the nation's third president, Thomas Jefferson was a farmer and a scientist who loved gadgets and invented some himself, including a cipher wheel to create secret messages in code. You can see them if you visit his home at Monticello in Virginia (monticello.org).

There's a special Slave Life tour that highlights the lives of the community who built and ran Mount Vernon. See where the slaves lived in the re-created slave cabin and the Slave Memorial. Six or more people would have lived in the small cabin, and the kids would have slept on the floor.

Do you wonder what the Washingtons ate for dinner? There's even a special tour that explains how food was prepared and served. There were no refrigerators then. Food was rolled in salt and spices and then smoked or dried. Visit the smokehouse.

You'll also want to visit the working blacksmith shop and the George Washington Pioneer Farmer site. You might be able to help with the harvest!

A VISITING KID SAYS:
"I liked seeing George Washington's kitchen; he had so many pretty pots."
—Sophia, 8, Long Beach, CA

{ **What's Cool?** The online Kids Zone for Colonial Williamsburg with games and a kid's-eye view of the 18th century (history.org/kids).

George Washington experimented with new crops and bred livestock to provide strong work animals (there were no tractors in those days, of course!) as well as to produce wool, leather, meat, milk, butter, and fertilizer. Nothing was wasted. Even horns were used—for toothbrushes.

See some of the breeds that George Washington raised—Hog Island sheep, Bronze Gobbler turkeys, Red Devon cattle, horses, mules, and oxen. They are friendly, so you can pet them! Check out the large stone gristmill he built to increase production of flour and cornmeal and the whiskey distillery next door. It was the largest in America, making George Washington a very successful entrepreneur as well as a farmer and statesman. In summer, there's usually a Hands-on-History tent near the mansion where you can try on colonial kids' clothes, play 18th-century games, and maybe even spin wool.

Ready to come back to the 21st century yet?

DID YOU KNOW?

The last battle of the Revolutionary War was at Yorktown Battlefield in Virginia. Today it's a national park where there are special activities for kids and you can even earn a junior ranger badge (nps.gov/york/forkids/beajuniorranger.htm).

Civil War Battlefields

Cheers rang out in the streets of Washington, DC on a July day in 1861 when the soldiers marched out in what was hoped would be the battle to end the Civil War.

War had started in 1861 after many years of conflict between the North and the South, mainly over the issue of slavery. After the election of President Abraham Lincoln, some southern states decided to separate from the Union and formed the Confederacy. Many people thought the entire Civil War would be decided by one big battle at the First Battle of Manassas.

People were so confident of victory that they brought picnics into the field to watch. It was a mistake.

The new Union recruits were soundly beaten by the Confederates on July 21, 1861, on fields overlooking Bull Run in Manassas, Virginia. When the battle was over, nearly 900 were dead and 3,000 wounded. The Second Battle of Manassas was the following summer and the Union Army lost again, paving the way for the South's first invasion of the North. You can visit **Manassas National Battlefield Park** (nps.gov/mana/historyculture/second-manassas.htm) and learn more about the famous clashes here and about the Civil War. Check out the huge cannons! Become a National Battlefield Park junior ranger here and take an active role in learning Civil War history.

The Historic Triangle

Ready for some time travel?

You can go back to Revolutionary War America—the 1700s—and even further just by visiting what's called the Historic Triangle of Virginia, about 3 hours south of Washington, DC. People call it "the Birthplace of American Democracy."

That's because our huge nation grew out of this tiny place in Virginia where Europeans, American Indians, and Africans first lived together (historyisfun.org).

The first permanent English settlers sent by the Virginia Company of London were at Jamestown in 1607. It wasn't easy. A lot of them died. You've probably heard the story of Captain John Smith and Pocahontas. She was a Powhatan Indian here; he was among the first settlers. You can visit **Historic Jamestowne** (historicjamestowne.org), where archaeologists are working to learn more about the life of those first settlers. You can learn more about the settlers and the Powhatans too—even boarding replicas of the ships that sailed here, exploring the colonists' fort, and visiting the Powhatan village.

Fast-forward to just before the Revolutionary War in **Colonial Williamsburg** (history.org/kids/visitus) and meet the people—the tradespeople, royalty, plantation owners, slaves, redcoats, militia, farmers, and, of course, colonial children. You might even run into George Washington, Thomas Jefferson, or Patrick Henry walking around the streets of Virginia's colonial capital just as they did more than 230 years ago. You can play colonial games (think you could roll a hoop?), join the militia, and even eat colonial food. You can dress as a colonial kid too.

If you think you'd have wanted to fight with George Washington, head to **Yorktown Battlefield** (nps.gov/yonb) where you can explore where the last major battle of the Revolutionary War took place in the fall of 1781. Visit the re-created Continental Army encampment where you can see what life was like for American soldiers—you can watch a military drill, see what an 18th-century doctor did, try out a soldier's tent, and even join an artillery crew to learn how they prepared a cannon to fire (historyisfun.org/Continental-Army-Encampment.htm).

Visit a 1780s farm and see what kids had to do to help their parents. They didn't have much time to play!

{ **What's Cool?** All of the roller coasters and other attractions at Busch Gardens Williamsburg (seaworldparks.com/en/buschgardens-williamsburg).

TELL THE ADULTS:

BEYOND DC

There is a lot to see beyond DC that families will love:

- **Old Town Alexandria,** just 6 miles from Washington, DC, is where you can board a tall ship, visit the Torpedo Factory Art Center, or take a Ghost & Graveyard Tour (800-388-9119; visitalexandriava.com).

- **Annapolis, Maryland,** is home to the US Naval Academy (come during Commissioning Week in late May and watch the dress parades—888-302-2852; visitannapolis.org) and is known for its sailing enthusiasts. There's one boat that offers Pirate Adventures on the Chesapeake (410-263-0002; chesapeakepirates.com).

- **Baltimore, Maryland** (800-282-6632; baltimore .org) is only an hour's drive or less from Washington, DC. Here's the place to visit the Inner Harbor. Besides going to the National Aquarium, board a historic ship (410-539-1797; historicships.org), catch a Baltimore Orioles game at Camden Yards and visit the Babe Ruth Birthplace and Museum (216 Emory St.;

410-727-1539; baberuthmuseum.com), eat crab cakes, and explore the American Visionary Art Museum that is one of the most unique anywhere (800 Key Hwy.; 443-244-1900; avam.org). Railroad buffs will want to stop at the Baltimore & Ohio Railroad Museum, at the site of the country's first train station (901 W. Pratt St.; 410-752-2490; borail.org); and after you've seen the Star-Spangled Banner at the Smithsonian, visit Fort McHenry National Monument (E. Fort Street) where Francis Scott Key was inspired as the British fired on Fort McHenry to write "The Star-Spangled Banner" (nps.gov/fomc).

- **Six Flags America** is 12 miles from DC with more than 100 rides, including the Hurricane Harbor water area in summer and at least eight major roller coasters (13710 Central Ave., Upper Marlboro, MD; 301-249-1500; sixflags.com).

- **Great Falls National Park** in Virginia (nps.gov/grfa) is less than 20 miles from Washington, DC with hiking trails along the waterfalls and on the Maryland side, the C&O Canal National Historical Park (nps.gov/choh).

- **Shenandoah National Park** (nps.gov/shen) in the Blue Ridge Mountains has 500 miles of hiking trails, 30 fishing streams, and more. Skyline Drive follows the main ridge of the Blue Ridge Mountains.

CONNECT THE DOTS!

Connect the dots to draw one of America's most important historical figures. After you finish draw in the eyes and mouth.

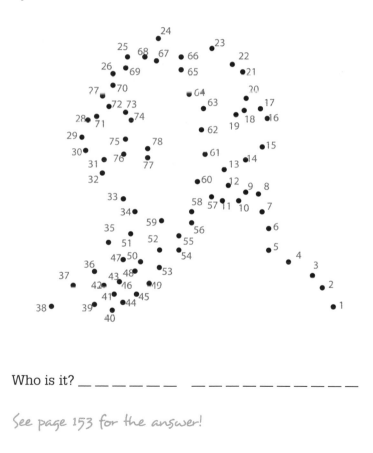

Who is it? _ _ _ _ _ _   _ _ _ _ _ _ _ _ _ _

See page 153 for the answer!

Index

Answer Keys

Washington, DC Word Scramble (p. 29)

1. Lincoln
2. Reflecting Pool
3. Martin Luther King Jr.
4. Eleanor Roosevelt
5. Washington
6. Arlington Cemetery
7. Cherry Blossoms
8. Kite Festival
9. Jefferson
10. World War II

Secret Code (p. 61)

"If this is coffee, please bring me some tea; if this is tea, please bring me some coffee."

White House Word Search (p. 75)

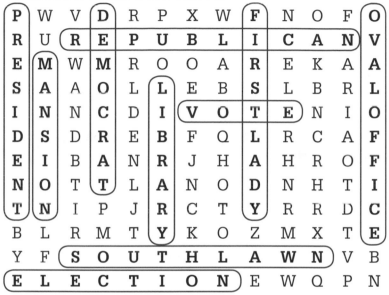

Get Outdoors Decoder (p. 129)

Rock Creek Park

Connect the Dots! (p. 145)

Who is it? George Washington

About the Author

Award-winning author Eileen Ogintz is a leading national family travel expert whose syndicated Taking the Kids is the most widely distributed column in the country on family travel. She has also created TakingtheKids.com, which helps families make the most of their vacations together. Ogintz is the author of seven family travel books and is often quoted in major publications such as *USA Today*, the *Wall Street Journal*, and the *New York Times*, as well as parenting and women's magazines on family travel. She has appeared on such television programs as *The Today Show*, *Good Morning America*, and *The Oprah Winfrey Show*, as well as dozens of local radio and television news programs. She has traveled around the world with her three children and others in the family, talking to traveling families wherever she goes. She is also the author of *The Kid's Guide to New York City* and *The Kid's Guide to Orlando* (Globe Pequot Press).